Memories of
My Life at the
College Valley

What I've Learned From Foxhounds
And The Men Who Hunt Them.

Martin Letts

Edited by John Strassburger

Order this book online at www.trafford.com
or email orders@trafford.com

Most Trafford titles are also available at major online book retailers.

Cover Photo: Martin Letts and the College Valley Hounds. (Jim Meads photo)

Printed in the United States of America.

ISBN: 978-1-4669-5439-7 (sc)
ISBN: 978-1-4669-5441-0 (hc)
ISBN: 978-1-4669-5440-3 (e)

Library of Congress Control Number: 2012917084

Trafford rev. 11/12/2012

 www.trafford.com

North America & international
toll-free: 1 888 232 4444 (USA & Canada)
phone: 250 383 6864 ✦ fax: 812 355 4082

CONTENTS

Foreword: Dennis J. Foster .... **vii**

Introduction: C. Martin Wood III, MFH.................**ix**

Preface .... **xvii**

1) A Day To Remember Forever............................**1**
And never to be repeated.

2) The Early Days..**4**
School life stoked my interest in field sports.

3) Breeding Hounds **10**
Partly science, largely art.

4) What I Like To See In A Hound **14**
Above all else, quality and perseverance.

5) Hound Exercise **17**
*It is second in importance only to breeding when
developing a pack.*

6) Hound Management..**21**
Practice close observation and implement fresh ideas.

7) Look To Out-Crossing 24
Inject hybrid vigor whenever possible—but never be satisfied with what you have.

8) Perseverance 35
A trait that forms the confidence of the hounds and the reputation of the huntsman.

9) Handling Hounds 38
Stamp your methodology to fulfill your ambitions.

10) Get Off To A Good Start 45
It will certainly boost the pack's morale.

11) Breeding Reminiscences 47
The men and hounds who've taught me the most.

12) Heaven Is Close 54
Especially on Holy Island.

13) Turn Of The Tide 56
A tale of misadventure at the heavenly host.

14) Robert's Fox 59
A hard frost revealed a memorable hunt, until darkness fell.

15) Baking Day 62
"Dispatch that fox, or you'll not eat!"

16) Raglan '66 64
My most brilliant hound.

FOREWORD

Martin Letts' brilliance for hunting and breeding foxhounds has been heretofore much confined to the crème de la crème of huntsmen and masters on both sides of the Atlantic. I'm sure much of the reason is his solitary, quiet personality, which has been focused on hunting, with little time or desire to blow his own horn. A man of few words, little patience and huge talent.

Benjamin Hardaway III and Marty and Daphne Wood did recognize his talents years ago, though, and they were the first to expose him to North America by bringing him over to judge hound shows and to speak. Marty and Daphne Wood deserve full credit for almost forcing Letts to share his knowledge with the rest of us through this book. They were concerned that we would lose the knowledge from one of the greatest (and yet little known) huntsmen and masters of our time. Letts deserves the recognition, and foxhunting would be the loser without *Memories of My Life At The College Valley*.

The leaders of the MFHA Foundation agreed it was a worthwhile project that would benefit all mounted foxhunting, regardless of country. However, none of this would have been possible had it not been for John Strassburger agreeing to compile and edit the raw manuscript. John's editorial expertise, combined with his knowledge of foxhunting, writing skills and ability to translate the "king's language" (Letts writes in an almost old-English style) into something that both English and American readers could understand was pure brilliance. The combination of Martin Letts' and John Strassburger's expertise make this a book all hunt staff and any serious foxhunter "must have."

Dennis J. Foster
Executive Director
MFHA Foundation
Author of "Whipper-in"

INTRODUCTION

For almost 50 years, the names Martin Letts and the College Valley and North Northumberland Hounds have been synonymous with the great sport they've provided in the extremely challenging country of Northern England and the Border country of Scotland.

The College Burn, a small river that flows out of the Cheviot Hills and ultimately into the North Sea, forms the College Valley. The country is marked by high hills (tors), steep hillsides, deep valleys and low heather. The hills will have heavy patches of bracken fern and gorse, which can run the whole distance from the valley floor to the top of the hill. Scattered throughout are big swatches of open scree slopes, bare shingle rock faces and huge piles of jumbled boulders (borrans), making the footing extremely treacherous for both hounds and horses. It is a wild, unforgiving country that can be made even more torturous by the wild weather the area is known for, as storms blow across the North Sea to break on the Cheviot Hills.

The country had a very large fox population, and so it has provided tremendous sport for the pack's followers. The high ground is predominately a sheep-farming country, while the low ground accommodates sheep, cattle and arable land. Most of the latter hunting country came to the College Valley Hounds when they amalgamated with the North Northumberland in the early 1980s.

Mark you that group that stands by the stell!
Here is no ponderous pride
Here is no swagger, no place for the swell,
But a handful of fellows who'll ride
A fox to his death over upland and fell
Where a hundred good foxes have died.

Here is the Master of Hounds—take note!—
On a rough horse run on the farm;
And here is the Whip in a rusty coat
With a terrier under his arm,
And a holloa hid in his rough red throat
To work hill-foxes harm.

From The Hill Men: Galloping Shoes Verses,
by Will H. Ogilvie (1923)

Martin was a young man when he took over the horn from Sir Alfred Goodson, who had bred the pack for almost forty years and turned it into one of the best packs of foxhounds in the world. Martin learned well at the master's side and has carried on his own breeding policies to improve the pack's already strong bloodlines and to create a very level pack of hill hounds, which combine the best attributes of the Fell hound and the modern English foxhound, with a dash of hound lines from America thrown in. A mark of the success of Martin's breeding program is the fact that College Valley bloodlines are used in many significant kennels in the United States and England, including my own Live Oak Hounds, where College Valley Trinket '69 remains the single predominant tail female line in our kennel today, after being first introduced in 1977.

And here is the pack, from their benches torn
Long ever the cock had crowed,
To follow the hint of the Master's horn through the
mist of the moorland road;
Half of them lame, with pads red-worn
On the screes where the shingle showed.

And here's the covert; no woodland wide
But a bunch of stunted whin—
A place where a mouse could hardly hide
Or a spider find room to spin.
The Master, up in his stirrups to ride,
Is cheering them 'Leu, boys, in!'

Will H. Ogilvie (1923)

I took a bit of poetic license with the previous quotation, in that Martin Letts would not knowingly hunt a lame hound. In fact, Martin's hounds are known for their sound, durable feet, which are the result of his careful selective breeding. The verse, however, paints the picture of the hounds moving off on a misty morning up the narrow lanes to the start of the upland fells, trotting along quietly with their huntsman toward the first draw. The College Valley country is not marked with nice discreet coverts, but rather with vast, open heather- and grass-covered hillsides stretching to the skyline, broken by patches of bracken fern, gorse and whins of stunted trees.

As the hounds are cast, they spread out up the hill, searching for the line of a fox, and they'll make their way into the most likely bits of cover available for a fox to lie up. The day then becomes mostly a continuous draw, as the hunt progresses from hillside to valley and then back again. It is most useful for the followers to get up high on the ridge to be able to see the action, as well as to save their horses for the gallop that must follow. I have honestly seen a RAF Harrier jet flying in the valley below me while hunting with the College Valley hounds on a brilliantly clear day.

Eventually, of course, the fox may well run out of the valley in which he's been found and, at that time, horses and riders can follow along the ridge, if they're lucky, or else have to go down the near side and up the far side again in order to stay in touch with hounds. It can be desperate riding, with the horses and riders well-winded by the time they achieve the distant ridge.

> Scarce have they quested a quarter through
>> With their sterns all waving gay,
> When the hills are rent with a hullabaloo
>> And the fellow they want is away
> A great hill-fox running right in view
>> With his mask to the Merlin Brae.
>
> Up by the glidders he glides and goes
>> To his stronghold under the scar,
> But a shepherd was there ere the sun-god rose
>> And his door shows bolt and bar,
> So he turns his head to the south; he knows
>> It is time to go fast and far.

Will H. Ogilvie (1923)

The College Valley hounds are known far and wide for their ability to hunt independently and yet to honor each other and get together quickly when one of them opens on a good line. It is an amazing sight to see the hounds working a line, opening on that line, and then all of them streaming across the open moorland as they hark to each other, come together as a pack to really start to hunt, and then run their fox. For all of their independence and Fell breeding, the College Valley hounds are an amazingly biddable pack, and that is one of the reasons that others have used their bloodlines so extensively. Many, like me, seek to produce a pack with nose, drive and cry that can hunt together under almost any conditions—steep hills, low grassy bogs, high winds, rain, sleet and snow, or bright sunshine with dry, dusty heather and grass.

> *Over the top come the lean white hounds*
> *Screaming to scent and view;*
> *The hills are waked to their furthest bounds*
> *As they clamor and drive him through*
> *And the joy of the far-flung challenge sounds*
> *Till it shivers against the blue.*
>
> *Then a clatter of hoofs. The Master first*
> *Crouched low on his cat-foot grey—*
> *'if we don't get him now in the first quick burst*
> *We'll be riding the hills all day!'*
> *Says the Whip, 'That's the cove from Brackenhurst*
> *That carried Bob's lambs away!'*

Will H. Ogilvie (1923)

Since Martin Letts hunts a sheep country, one of the services that the College Valley performed for its landowners and tenants was predator control, and, make no mistake, the big hill foxes are serious predators of young sheep and lambs, especially during lambing time in the spring of the year. To perform their job, the hounds must be absolutely steady to sheep, as well as to the red deer, roe deer, hares and rabbits that also inhabit the moors and fells. Martin and his predecessor, Sir Alfred Goodson, have developed a type of hound that exhibits the intelligence to learn very quickly as young hounds what the appropriate quarry is and then to stick to it, to the exclusion of other forms of riot.

> *'Faith and it is!' Bob, riding blind,*
> *Comes slithering over the screes,*
> *His pony now on its fat behind*
> *And now on its battered knees—*
> *'He had legs as long as a foal, I mind,*
> *And a trunk as big as a tree's.'*
>
> *Says Bill: 'There's a stranger stuck in the bog*
> *With nowt, but his head in sight,*
> *And there he may lie like a drain-fast Hogg*
> *Till the hounds come back at night.*
> *Look he, man Dave, at yon old white dog*
> *Going over the top—yon's right!'*
>
> *A holloa breaks from the hills ahead*
> *And an answering 'For'ard on!'*
> *There's a clatter down in the burn's rough bed:*
> *Then the mist drops weird and wan;*
> *The rubble rings to a clinking tread*
> *Far off—and the hunt is gone.*

Will H. Ogilvie (1923)

In my mind, Will Ogilvie's lovely verses do more to convey what it was like to hunt with Martin Letts and his College Valley hounds than any scribbling that I could do on a sheet of foolscap. It captures the essence of hunting with this marvelous pack of hill hounds, with all of the rough country, desperate gallops, brilliant scenery and views, and, most importantly, the camaraderie of the chase as it was practiced by Martin and his lovely wife and joint-master, Eildon.

I had the privilege of hunting with them on more than one occasion, and I have frequently visited the kennels to look at hounds and to judge their annual puppy show. There is fellowship, warmth, camaraderie and a general sense of marvelous people pulled together by the sport that they love and by this wonderful pack of hounds.

Martin Letts anchors all of the hunting at the College Valley. Until he stepped down from his position as huntsman in 2003, Martin had hunted and bred the College Valley for nearly fifty years. His knowledge of hounds and their hunting and breeding may be paralleled by a few, but is surpassed by none.

In addition to his knowledge of venery and of the sport, Martin is quite a character himself. When first met, Martin comes across as being gruff, short on words and suffering no fools lightly. As you get to know him, though, you quickly become the target of his quick wit and sharp sense of humor. The best thing that my wife, Daphne, and I have found to do when suffering the slings and arrows of his Northumbrian style is to give back as good as we get. That will always elicit a smile and a crinkling of eyes from Martin, and the conversation can then go on to know no bounds whatsoever.

Despite his gruff exterior, Martin Letts is a warm and friendly man who delights in imparting his vast font of knowledge to anyone sincerely interested. I have had many wonderful conversations sitting before the fire with a glass of malt at hand, discussing not only hounds and their breeding, but also hunting in general. Martin is a pillar of knowledge on our sport and a good raconteur of events that have marked his hunting life and the last half a century of foxhunting in England. When he turned over the horn to his joint-master Ian

McKie, latterly of the Bicester and Whaddon Chase, Martin Letts was the longest-serving active master and huntsman of hounds in the British Isles.

This treatise that he has developed for foxhunters is a great example of knowledge meeting pen and paper. It will stand the test of time as a way for the "expert," as well as the novice, to get a grasp of the issues to be faced when building, developing and hunting a cracking pack of foxhounds. Martin has hunted with me both while I was carrying the horn and since I've been forced to follow hounds mounted aboard my "Steel Stallion." Each time, we would sit and quietly discuss the day and the performance of both the huntsman and the hounds. And, each time, by the end of our quiet words with each other, I would walk away with a new bit of useful knowledge that could be put to work immediately to improve my pack's performance in the field.

That is the essence of *Memories of My Life At The College Valley*, and I hope that readers will attempt to glean the important messages incorporated in it. Martin Letts, MFH, has done a great service for the sport of foxhunting, and his words will ring true for many generations. Daphne and I feel privileged to have counted Martin and Eildon Letts as close friends for many decades.

Tally-Ho Forever

C. Martin Wood III, MFH
Live Oak Hounds
December 2012

PREFACE

This book is my attempt to promote sound hunting tactics in varied country, in country where hounds have to be independent to achieve success, and especially where funds are limited.

Most hunting practices stem from the traditional hunting territories of England, but outside these areas, particularly overseas, countries often have sterner territory and a wide variation in weather patterns. Thus the usual hunting treatises often did not make allowance for this. So when challenged by Marty and Daphne Wood of the Live Oak to write my hunting experiences for the Masters of Foxhounds Association of America, I rose to the challenge in the hope that I would balance Ben Hardaway's book *Never Outfoxed* by way of a more average tactical performance!

For my English readers, I emphasize that all my hunting experiences relate to a time period prior to February 1, 2003.

My book, apart from technical advice, is interspersed with hunting memories of my career in that sport, which I hope readers do not find as a misalliance of reminiscence and unshared geography.

Circumstance and luck dropped me—a very square peg—into a very square hole when hunting was back in a full recovery situation following the Second World War. Those with whom I worked were high in breeding and kennel management. The Evans family came from Wales, and two generations gave great service to the College Valley between

1924 until 1986, when Andrew Proe joined and continued those standards and more until the present day. Continuity in any sphere is of great importance, but in my experience particularly in hunting.

My family—particularly Eildon, my wife, and Diana, my daughter—have given me great support over the years, even when that loyalty was fully exploited by long waits at earths in windy places or when a short fuse was examined at the fireside.

I am grateful also to Tessa Waugh, who has translated a rheumatic hand into decipherable copy.

Martin Letts
December 2012

Chapter 1

A Day To Remember Forever

And never to be repeated.

A utumn hunting can be unpredictable, as can scenting conditions, but October 1, 1990, was a clear, still morning with a good dew and a hint of frost in the air. We had a sporting day in front of us, because we were due to meet at Mindrum Mill, a mixed grass and arable farm on the edge of the hills, at 8:00 a.m. The farm was owned by a staunch foxhunter who maintained a renowned privet and gorse covert known as Mindrum Whin, which always contained a stout litter of cubs. Furthermore, at 12 noon, the Dummer Beagles, on their annual visit to Northumberland, were meeting just above Hethpool in College Valley, and at the end of the day they were expected in for tea at Hethpool—a traditional end to their holiday.

At Mindrum, after a welcome from Rosalie Chartres, a large field of foxhunters and beaglers assembled on the crags above the famous covert, and the hounds were soon engaged with a strong litter in the immediate vicinity. After some 15 minutes, about half the pack went away with a good cry in the direction of the Bowmont Water. As this was obviously the line of a seasoned fox, whipper-in Andrew Proe's instruction from myself was to "stop 'em!" and bring them back to the Whin, something he achieved with difficulty. The morning continued well but somewhat inconclusively, as scent disintegrated in the warm autumn sunshine. The final draw was the old cemetery, and hounds ran better back to the meet. Here there was some confusion as the vast majority of our field were re-loading their horses after a long, hot morning, some with the prospect of beagling and then tea at Hethpool.

During this melee our fox surmounted the garden wall and with a disdainful swish of his brush made back for the Whin. The volume of cry quickly confirmed this was our early morning customer, and in the long hunt that ensued, hounds only checked twice—a 6 ½-mile point to the Tweed in Buccleugh territory, a sharp southward turn at Kersquarter instantly righted by Watchman, to turn back to College Valley country on Wide-Open Farm—16 ½ miles in 1 ½ hours, a burning scent indeed.

My terrier man passed me on a lane in his truck, and both of us were aware that the large earths on Wide-Open were unstopped—a likely refuge for a tiring fox. "Try and get there before him" was my instruction. After a fall from my horse, which I deserved by giving him an unnecessary reminder for speed, Eildon (my wife) and Diana (my daughter) held open a gate—and we were alone in contact with the hounds. As we topped the ridge, we spotted Andrew the terrier man's vehicle in key position and the hounds driving on beyond the earths—a relief, as success now seemed inevitable. However, when we came up with Andrew, he reported that hounds got up to the fox in the covert beyond, but he had turned short back to find the last hole open.

After such a splendid performance, who could begrudge this fox his victory, especially in view of our imminent social responsibilities? We, therefore, made a hurried trip home and put all hands to the plough, with sandwich spreading and kettle boiling, to put tea on the table with a minute to spare.

Robin Leach, master of the Dummer, was ecstatic about his day—three hares accounted for and all good hunts. I lay back on the sofa with a bruised rear and twisted ankle, nodding vaguely but appreciatively at the details of his day with a very large whisky to aid digestion thereof.

Our memorable day's hunt was written up and appeared in the *Horse And Hound* adjacent to the Exmoor, who had "an excellent morning with three accounted for," inscribed with the well-known lettering R.E.W. [Ronald E. Wallace] following the hunting report. Our hunt made it all small beer! The telephone rang one Sunday, and the caller observed, "It seems you have had rather a good hunt." Praise from the direction of "heaven" was not to be lightly dismissed!

Even today, a trip to Kelso on the road that the fox crossed and re-crossed still awakens memories of that hunt with its twists and turns, along with the vagaries of autumnal scenting. But, alas, we never met up with that fox again—nor was such a run repeated in that countryside in my career as a huntsman.

Chapter 2

The Early Days

School life stoked my interest in field sports.

My father attended a public school, Marlborough, and despite the difficulties of travelling immediately after the Second World War, this tradition was followed for my brother and for me. It was a wonderful school for a prospective countryman since it encouraged its pupils' interest in sport and a range of interests and hobbies. To the east lay Savernake Forest, the second-largest area of a Norman royal forest, laid out for hunting the red deer in those times. The River Kennet—a renowned chalk stream—flowed through its environs and was full of wary, corpulent brown trout, so fishing within school grounds was available to staff and pupils.

The contents of the school library included Grey's *Flyfishing* and *The Charm of Birds*, which encouraged boys' interest in country affairs. To the west lay unspoilt downland, manicured in part for racehorse gallops but mostly ancient grassland, close-cropped by sheep and an ideal environment for the many varieties of birds and butterflies so well described by Richard Jefferies in his books. Perhaps the most-thumbed title was *The Amateur Poacher,* for post-war food in the college dining hall was not wide enough in variety for schoolboys who were used to living on farms in the countryside.

Thus a clique of eight or ten boys got together and developed their fielding abilities between wickets by catching rabbits and moor hens for the pot, in the water meadows, by means of slight of hand or with ferrets and purse-nets kept illicitly in the Natural History Society building situated just outside the college. In the early autumn term, brown trout journeyed upstream to the higher reaches of the Kennet to feed on water shrimps, and they gave away their presence at our water by eruptions in the weeds to regain deeper pools. The capture of pink-fleshed trout of three to four pounds greatly tickled schoolboy appetites. Such a catch also tickled the appetites of housemasters, who needed to be sensitized to the unorthodox activities of a sporting minority of their pupils.

Hunting books played an important role in developing this interest, and visits to the local Tedworth Hunt were encouraged since bicycling was regarded a suitable exercise for boys. Mr. Gough taught English literature to the lower school and was a hunting man himself, keeping a horse at livery and riding out on Saturdays. He was no bold rider, and he preferred the rides of Savernake Forest, complete in black coat and top hat. One sharp hunt in the trees lost him his hat—and the ginger wig beneath it—to a low-slung branch. The confidentiality of this episode was lost when the master's teenage daughter galloped to the front of the field to announce, "Daddy, Daddy, Mr. Gough has been scalped!"

George Goodwin was the huntsman, and, like many of his profession, he was a kind man, adept in nursing schoolboy interest in hounds and their care and in the whereabouts of cubs. The Pewsey Vale and the downs tested his ability in the field, and the Savernake Forest and the West Woods tested his perseverance. The lighter moments for vulgar boys came when George rose in his stirrups and watered a bramble bush at considerable range from his saddle, and I have never witnessed a man who could improve on this particular skill.

To the west of the Tedworth country lay the Duke of Beaufort's Thursday country, and one day the school grapevine revealed that this pack was due to meet at Cliffe Pypard, some 10 miles west of Marlborough. Thus an expedition was implemented, and six boys pedalled exuberantly to arrive at the roadside gorse covert just as George Read found his afternoon fox. It had been a difficult morning, after a white frost and bright sunshine, and it continued so. But it was ideal for the small party to keep in touch with the hounds, who hunted a short-running fox with accuracy and deep cry. With a returning frost and an improving scent we were outpaced, and so we retrieved our bicycles, abandoned in a ditch, to report to the College gatekeeper by 6:30. But we had brought back with us a deep impression, firmly ingrained on my memory, of a great pack, well handled.

The day had immediate repercussions in that during evening revision came an urgent summons from my housemaster. Sneyd had not returned, and his housemaster felt obliged to mount a search party since it was snowing heavily. Would I venture out with him since I knew the route we had taken? Anything was better than revision, but we had hardly gone a mile before I spotted a tottering, snow-covered figure in the headlights. "There's your man," I directed, "and that will save you a bereavement letter to the ever-loving." Mr. Knight reported back to my housemaster that Letts had been helpful but was somewhat callous in make-up. Sneyd recovered and became an officer in the Royal Engineers and master of their drag hounds, although he always exhibited a marked reluctance to hunt in wintry conditions!

My friends Nick Wykes and James Bouskell and I had ambitions to start a Beagle pack at Marlborough, and the essentials were in place until the headmaster developed transfer ambitions and was reluctant to saddle his successor with such a political innovation before arrival. Fortunately Mr Garnett was a supporter and the spadework fell in place for Wykes and Bouskell, who became masters and huntsman.

I thought my hunting education would be better advanced by whipping-in to the Bolebroke, whose mastership had developed a distinguished pack since 1934 and whose huntsman was Tom Moran, a man whose experience was wide in foxhunting and otter hunting, as well as beagling.

After two years of national service, I returned to civilian life a wiser man, eager to extend my experience in the chase, as well as to develop appropriate skills for the family business.

Tom Moran was a genius at kennel management, and he developed a greatly detailed control of hounds, but perhaps his hounds lacked enterprise. He was, however, the perfect foil for an ambitious amateur who desired that enterprise but also instant response in his hounds. I was given an opportunity to hunt the hounds on a bye day in March 1957. Tom climbed a tree to give me the sole attention of the hounds, but they winded his position and sang around its trunk—an absolutely inauspicious start.

The following year both Tom and Phil Burrows were lame, so I carried the horn on Christmas Eve. No singing around the tree for me, but a good hunt and the hare caught in the next parish. For the next six seasons I hunted hounds on Saturdays and on any weekdays that I could secure from work commitments. I also explored the backwaters of Norfolk, Suffolk and Essex by hunting the Eastern Counties Otterhounds, a pack of mixed variety—the Otterhound, the Old English, modern English and Welsh, and the Crossbred. It was at the Eastern Counties that I encountered the best hound I handled, however: Deacon, a draft from the Cambridge Drag with Dumfries blood about him.

The experience also taught me how to communicate with a wide range of countrymen, keepers, water bailiffs, pest officers and poachers, all of whom "knew" the whereabouts of the quarry and its habits.

Visiting for a week or so of hunting was the social tradition, allowing exploration of rivers from Cornwall to Lancashire and practice at how best to balance woodcraft and alcoholic pressures!

However, the highlight of the sporting year, from 1958 onwards, was the Beagles' fortnightly visit to the hills of Northumberland, promoted by invitation of Col. Leonard Gibson, master of the Newcastle and District Beagles.

Early mornings up in the hills allowed the hounds to drag up to their hare after they'd fed at night on outlying fields, and then hunt at pace over the heather and heaths, with only sheep foil as a difficulty. This timetable also allowed visits to local foxhounds—the Percy, West Percy and College Valley—and different Beagle packs, all of which enjoyed the colonel's generosity.

The Bolebroke enjoyed a late meet at the Tower Hotel, which was our base, an opportunity to show a crowd of sportsman what our hounds could achieve. One year our stay at this base was endangered when Tom acquired a piglet from the Newcastle flesh house, cleaned it up and adorned it in the receptionist's nightgown, complete with bonnet, and then placed it in her bed. Subsequent hysterics awoke the hotel and led to my expulsion to the servant's quarters. But it was a punishment not without advantage, for I was first in line for early morning tea and other favours supplied by the younger female staff.

By the early '60s, my knowledge of the country and the habits of the hill hare was deep, and in 1962 a spell of settled weather produced a period of vintage sport. As luck transpired, this coincided with a trip north by Bill Browne, master and huntsman of the Portman from 1920 to 1939. At the end of the week Sir Alfred and Lady Goodson had asked Bill and his wife to lunch at Corbet Tower. Emboldened by a glass of Port, I asked Bill to give me a recommendation as a young man about to move north with a branch of the Letts business. Thus was simply struck my long and happy association with the College Valley and the Goodson family, a justification that luck has an undeniable part to play in hunting.

Chapter 3

Breeding Hounds

Partly science, largely art.

B reeding foxhounds is a fascinating aspect of our sport that is restricted to a few masters, even though some members of the field do follow it with interest. The fruits of breeding hounds are a comparatively short-term realisation compared to other species, since maturity is quick and performance over a variety of skills is apparent sixty times a season—frequent enough for even a newcomer to draw conclusions. Improvement in conformation is also apparent at puppy shows, due to hounds' rapid maturity of physique.

Ikey Bell's book *A Huntsman's Logbook* is a book that repays study for those interested in hound breeding, for, although it is based on times past, it focuses on the priorities for accurate assessment of working abilities, provides details on conformation that is vital toward that end, and emphasises the importance family lines play in hastening gains in performance. Modern life does not render practical the degree of study that enabled Bell to contribute so much to hunting, but it should concentrate the minds of modern breeders to give every attention to the achievements of individual hounds, both in home kennels and farther afield. The spirit of helpful assistance is still present today, as much as in the past, especially as modern conditions provide extra challenges in proving the merit of our hounds. Every breeder should start out with the confidence that he or she has a contribution to make, but with the realization of the time scale over which their efforts will have to be concentrated.

The skill of the breeder is to cement the hunting abilities of his hounds (abilities that are exposed by regular and frequent work) by intelligently selecting the sire and dam. An easy phrase to write, but no straightforward task to implement. In my chapter on out-crossing (Chapter 7), I note how quickly Playfair '63 injected improvements to the hunting style of the pack as a whole. Animals, especially those in tight communities like a pack, recognize success and dominance, and they respond speedily to it by following others' examples, especially when encouraged by their huntsman. At risk of repetition, I advance the opinion that often a huntsman's attention is too focused on the hounds at the head of the pack, especially when crossing a ride or road in woodland country. However, the hound that excels in every aspect of the chase—the finder, the accurate hunter, the one that reinstates the hunt—and displays these attributes consistently on nearly ever day in the season is the dog or bitch most worthy of breeding.

Accurate assessment is the prime attribute for any successful breeder of stock, especially if they are objective about their home produce and are generous to neighboring packs of merit. Assessment at home should entail assistance from your staff and local countrymen whose opinion you respect. At the building stage of a breeding program, a season's experience will establish obvious options. Putting a sound home dog to your best bitch is a good basis if pedigree lines are not overly close and the female line in kennel is well established. However, back up this choice by a selection of a sire or dam from a pack whose performance most meets your ambitions and whose country is similar to your own. There are two options to this: service of a dog of your choice whose performance in the field is vouched for by their huntsman and whose ancestry is likewise distinguished, or loan of a bitch to take a litter from. I have used both, but if your kennel lacks established female lines, the second is the way to go forward if your eventual ambition is to have a "typey" pack.

If the outside dog of your choice is in much demand, do not pass by his less fashionable brother; the genes are the same and good looks are a transient quality. If your selection produces what you need, then return to the same kennel again to inherit the levelness of their pack and to reinforce their working attributes. In the interests of a wide gene pool, explore at least one reserve breeding option. Foxhounds can be careless mothers and, if aged, a foster bitch is sound insurance for a bad-milking dam. While a good-mothering bitch can raise a large number of whelps, remember that an overly large family can restrict your future breeding options.

A well-balanced pack that has representation from every year's entry, up to the sixth season, is an important middle-term objective. Shortage of a particular age, while no short-term disadvantage, may develop into a serious disadvantage if your drafting for working standards has to be severe.

A large entry in a single year can imbalance the experience factor, especially as the young hounds acquire fitness and reach the "know-all" stage. To go into a season with a large new entry, when second-season hounds are short of working experience, is a grave risk to the effectiveness of the pack as a whole, even if the handlers are highly experienced. Working standards are quickly lost but long to regain.

Once you have acquired an established pack, I regard it a common-sense policy to arrange at least one litter in each entry that is so independent in bloodlines as to secure the practicality of an in-house solution in each year of entry. If you have a successful breeding year, be generous with drafts or gifts of whelps, for by means of reciprocation you can sustain lines of value in times of difficulty on your own.

If you feel a certain cross meets with high success, be wary of exact repetition in future seasons. It is my experience that the value of a repeat alliance is not often fully rewarded (the human race excluded). Hounds have varied maturing rates, and the precocious are more than often overtaken by their later-maturing littermates. Horse racing emphasizes well how form influences breeding results, and hounds are similar, especially bitches, where menstrual timing is a factor. A lay-off, not speedy drafting, is the solution, and patience is often rewarded, especially if the genes are there.

Stamina is the last attribute to mature in horse or hound, and over-exercising it can blunt enthusiasm for quite a time, so do not exploit the merit of your best young hounds by over-hunting them.

The advantage claimed for a well-bred pack is that merit of performance is well spread throughout the pack. Through standards of conformation, the pack arrives at a moment of difficulty carrying a tight head, so then the specialists are close up to the drivers, and they can resolve the problems of a check quickly. Followers of such a pack seldom resort to the well-oiled excuse of a bad-scenting time, as their hounds remain in close contact with their quarry while maintaining the pace of a hunt. I have been lucky in that respect over much of my career, but I have noted when the merit of an individual hound is much exalted, the performance of the remainder of the pack is seldom meritorious.

The skills of the breeder and of the huntsman have much in common. Although methodology plays its part for each one, great success for each depends upon flair. Act upon instinct, and you will be rewarded.

Chapter 4

What I Like To See In A Hound

Above all else, quality and perseverance.

W hen evaluating hounds on the flags, quality depends upon a skeletal structure combining the pace and stamina points in unexaggerated harmony and natural balance. In other words, when not poised to the biscuit or at ease, you very seldom catch a quality hound in awkward stance.

A personal preference is a hound that is dark of nose and eye and has distinctive marking over the saddle or pelvis, finishing short of the shoulder, to naturally accentuate its quality. Length of neck is also a contributor, but the essentials of the shoulder are the length of humerus, which provides stride, and the angle of the scapula, which if overly vertical contributes to a jarring stride and to lack of fluidity in movement. Muscle strength in the pelvis is key to a powerful connection between front and hind limbs, and the key to this, in a mature hound, is that the knobs of the spine are encased by muscle development, so are not apparent to the eye.

Length between hip and hock is a pace indicator, just as an angled hock and muscle at the stifle as are indicators of power behind the saddle. I also look for width in the pelvis to allow natural thrust and to allow the hind limbs to pass to the outside of the front limbs at top pace. I look for depth, but not coarseness, at the heart, and for the front rib to descend to the elbow point but without width to obstruct the swing of limb movement.

I want to see fluidity in movement, with the step up in pace developing from length of stride and elasticity, rather than celerity of limb movement.

A well-set stern and a masculine jaw set are two more preferences, as an undershot jaw is a prepotent fault.

Good looks will influence pride in display and lead to cockiness in the individual and jealousy within the pack. An obvious preventative when displaying your stars is to hold a general "all in" for the whole pack, so overall quality is displayed and opportunity for jealousy removed. When displaying hounds at a show, keep your stars separate till feeding time next morning, for, as with humans, a missed outing creates jealousy.

In the kennel, I look for a hound that is social and kind to his companions and respectful of his seniors. He should be playful in the grass yard, but, if put in a corner, he should stand up for his rights. A cocky young dog will soon come to heel when shut in alone with one of the pack's lead dogs.

Hounds should be affectionate with the staff, but they should have the ability to accept a reprimand without sulkiness or moodiness. They should be full of dash and enthusiasm on exercise, but swift to react to command.

Hounds should best be neither a glutton nor a picky feeder at the trough, and they should soon become a schoolmaster on the couples. A hound should recall his puppy walker with exuberance but be disdainful of farm stock and other dogs after initial introduction.

In the field, I look for a sure rather than a precocious starter, a hound who is quick to learn right from wrong. I want a natural tryer in all aspects of the chase and an enthusiast throughout the day, even in unhelpful conditions. I want a hound who does his turn throughout the season without undue loss of condition. If a hound does lose condition through lack of maturity, I give him a break. I find this is usually enough, for the tough sort will quickly be restored, and with added enthusiasm. However, if a late litter does not respond, I put them by till their second season. Never overdo young hounds, especially in hot conditions, for enthusiasm is not always a permanent condition.

In the second season, muscle development and hunting ability should come with maturity, so that at season's end, a youngish hound of merit should be running at head and playing a part in regaining initiative at the check. The development of a good hound into a great hound depends much on the skill of the huntsman and his judgement to mix assistance and self-reliance, thus contributing perseverance in abundance—a quality essential for a great pack of hounds.

Chapter 5

Hound Exercise

It is second in importance only to breeding when developing a pack.

When I took over the College Valley in 1964, hound exercise was limited to a two to three times per week. Once a certain level of fitness was reached, it was remarked by one of my tutors, "If you take them out more, they will break away and go hunting without you."

But in 1967 there was a serious outbreak of foot-and-mouth disease, and all hunting was closed down in England between November 1st and February 1st. I exercised my pack between those dates on a bicycle on all convenient days without trouble, and on the first Tuesday of the start of hunting they proved to be fitter than the local foxes. We caught a brace after short hunts and then caught a good fox after a fine hunt of almost two hours. As I rather smugly took off the brush and placed it in the tail pocket of my hunting coat, a sharp hound noted the disappearance of this trophy and seized it and my right index finger at the same time. Almost 45 years later, I still have the mark of it to remind me of that day—and the importance of hound exercise!

Top sportsmen pay a fortune for a good coach, and they change them whenever results are less than satisfactory.

Think of the huntsman as the pack's coach. Hound exercise is essential for discipline, and, if well executed, it plays a part in developing questing or drawing for the quarry, casting, working as a close-knit team, and equality of fitness and condition. Every huntsman of merit will have his measure of how he assesses ideal control in the hunting field, and this will vary according to the type of country he hunts, the variety of hound he favors, and his own style of handling.

To a sportsman's eye there are three characteristics of a gun dog whenever his handler discusses the prospects for the day with his fellow guns. The first is the one who plonks himself down at the gun's feet and gazes rapturously at his master's face. The second is the one who soon rakes off to put up a pheasant from a nearby hedge, and the third is the one who remains standing, alert and on the verge of control, but returns on a word from his master. If I go to a meet and sense a pack exhibiting the characteristic of the last, I shall think the chances of a good day are at optimum.

The indicators of a high-class pack of hounds in the field are their ability to draw, their ability to cast, and their ability to run up together. Hound exercise, if properly executed, can contribute to the foundations of all these qualities, although the primary objective remains fitness. Short-range control is marching at a hound jog at attention—a man in front or a man behind—and control by name and not by using the whip "as a fishing rod."

When exercising hounds, I aim to have more than one route to follow and to have a place for hound relaxation, where a fuss can be made of the introverted or those that have been cautioned for misdemeanors. Couples are a useful preliminary tool and a good signal of demotion after bad behavior. A month of short exercise will do wonders for discipline and for the conformation of the young hounds, especially if progress is not always "forward, march," but with byways and gateways explored and long-range control developed. Junctions, of roads or lanes, should simulate trickery, so if hounds attempt to follow yesterday's route, take the alternative and give them a late word so they rejoin you flustered and with peer disapproval. This routine should be further explored in the fields with more license.

All this is an important rung in the ladder to developing hounds' ability for casting and drawing, for by so doing you are developing the hounds' eye for the direction changes by their huntsman. Through regular exercise, all this can be achieved by a quiet, encouraging word and controlled collective movement, with the hounds on their noses, rather than by emphatic and noisy commands that raise heads and break concentration.

Hounds will meet a variety of animals in the hunting field, but they should first meet as many as possible in the disciplined environment of exercise. If young hounds show an unhealthy interest in farm animals, hold them up until introduction stimulates boredom and, only then, move on.

Hounds can immediately recognize when they've lost your full attention. When a social call is necessary, ensure that your whipper-in fills the attention gap at all times. This is especially important at a meet, when hounds may be kicked by fit and eager horses. Consequently, I like to say that people who wish to talk to both the huntsman and the whipper-in do not deserve a good day's sport.

Hound exercise on a summer morning is a delight, with hounds on their toes, yet responsive. On occasion, this exercise can be shared with friends, but schooling needs constant refreshing, and on a majority of days exercise should be confined to the professionals.

There will be the odd day when discipline disintegrates, and when that happens, take hounds home. If you do, you will find natural order is restored on the morrow.

Ensure that fitness coincides with the start date of hunting and does not precede it. Work toward that date, and if you conclude that the hounds' education is not complete, another week's delay for further education is not time misspent. Hounds should enjoy exercise, so don't overdo it, and discipline should stem from desire to please rather than fear of reprisal. To achieve this, the whipper-in must ration the rate with encouragement.

Even when you think you have achieved all your training objectives, never relax—the goddess Diana dislikes complacency, as I was once reminded while riding home when all seemed close to perfection. On a lose rein, within a quarter-mile of the kennels, a blackbird exploded from a hedgerow with a spluttered alarm call. My horse's exaggerated shy threw me onto the pommel of my saddle, with unpleasant pressure to a delicate spot, with result that an explosion of wrath caused an untidy bolt for the kennel!

Chapter 6

Hound Management

Practice close observation and implement fresh ideas.

One of my first childhood memories is a considerable battle of wills with my nanny, who was a dour Scot called Fraser, over a white linen sun hat she had selected for me to wear on a hot summer's day. Most unfortunately, after many tears and screams, I won this battle, and consequently in later life developed the awkward attributes of independence and obstinacy, and not only on headgear! I believe it is generally accepted that the characteristics developed in youth are influenced by the experiences of childhood, and this also applies to all animals of intelligence.

The management of hounds in kennel is, therefore, crucial to success in the field. Although the skills of good practice are best left to professional staff, the master who is hunting hounds (and, thus, responsible for sport) must have a basic knowledge of its science, for, regardless of the skill of the professional, the master is qualified in supervision to keep him up to the mark. My experience in such matters developed from establishments where economy demanded a single man as staff, augmented by amateur help, and my knowledge developed from observation of methodology and from my own help in holiday periods. The master hunting hounds should develop an open mind on kennel management and seek to introduce fresh ideas where necessary.

Development of the hound can start with weaning at six weeks of age. The primary principle of feeding should be little and often, for overfeeding can mar skeletal development at the green-stick stage of bone growth. Close observation at feeding time is a must throughout the hound's life, particularly in the early stages. Health and a desire for food are closely connected, and whelps can swing very quickly between health and sickness. The feeding routine should be regular and should, I believe, include withdrawal of the food dish on completion. Rearing puppies on a "help-yourself" basis encourages the picky feeder and complicates the first step of discipline. This can be implemented on food bribery, thus encouraging movement from grass yard to kennel or vice versa.

I hate to see legs of flesh available to whelps. Raw flesh is indigestible, devoid of tonic for the young, and usually unsustainable when the whelp goes out to his or her puppy walker. A change of diet is traumatic to the young, so half a sack of traditional food is a good present to a keen walker. Can I stress that it is my experience that a good start in the life of young hounds is almost as valuable as a good start in the making of a hunt?

Parasitic control routine is vital and should be checked by those supervising kennel management. I recall a story of a lady drinking in an English pub who withdrew after overhearing 15 minutes of conversation between two huntsmen. The politest of the pair expressed the hope that she had not been offended by their conversation. "No," she replied, "but if I had stayed longer, I felt I would be either wormed or served!" Their choice of location might have been faulty, but the subject matter was well chosen!

The ideal walk for a puppy is a rural one, where freedom and contact with children and farm stock is practical. Life within an outside run and controlled exercise and contact with horses is second best to ideal. A substantial grass yard, with a holding shelter at the kennels, is a very successful substitute practiced in the USA, where puppy walking is usually not possible. It is a formula that allows early handling discipline to develop when the hounds' learning capabilities are at their peak.

If a hound is kept confined and unhandled at this learning stage, I believe that he will probably never compete with his well-walked brothers or sisters in the field. Once in from walk, the young hound will need a week or three to acclimatize to kennel routine. Although the timing coincides with the pressures of the regular hunting season, it is a mistake to let the development of new arrivals be neglected for long.

To ensure steady development, feeding should be varied to match the development of the hound, and, therefore, "drawing" the hounds to the trough or the flesh is a crucial part of the kennel routine. It is important to achieve this process in orderly fashion, without undue noise or stick. Unless it can be done well, shy hounds do not feed well, the glutton gets more than is good for him, and the feeding time is lengthy. Methods to achieve this are best practiced outside feeding time, by moving the hounds from a lodge to a yard by calling their names.

As the process develops, control should be as long range as kennel geography allows and achieved on voice command, not by driving them like sheep. Thus, at the season's start, you will have a handy pack in kennel that will respond to the routine and discipline of hound exercise like fish to water.

Chapter 7

Look To Out-Crossing

Inject hybrid vigor whenever possible—but never be satisfied with what you have.

My justification for out-crossing hounds is connected to two sound fundamentals that were drummed into me by Bill Goodson, a man renowned for success in breeding many varieties of stock: First, never be satisfied by what you have achieved in breeding, and, second, the importance of injecting hybrid vigor into long-established lines, whether human or canine! These were two maxims he had already proven over 40 years of practice, over many generations of hounds, before I appeared on the scene.

The College Valley was, of course, founded on this basis. Goathland Rosebud '21, with Warwickshire roots, was line-bred to sons of Border Stormer '19, a dog who had made his mark on Goodson by accounting for his fox single-handed in a pigsty after that pack had ridden home following a long hunt. The progeny of this mating proved very successful, particularly in the attribute of perseverance, and so they encouraged close mating over the next two or three generations to establish a type. In the '30s young hounds were often purchased at hound sales to balance the casualties of distemper, and Lord Joicey, at the neighboring North Northumberland, acquired Frederick '36 as a whelp. On maturity, he was considered too plain for use at his new home, but he caught Goodson's eye for performance and tongue.

Upon research, he proved to be a grandson of the renowned hound Carmarthen Nimrod '28, whose line found favor at Badminton and Portman. Mated to a grand-daughter of Rosebud '21, she produced a fine litter, including the handsome dog Racer '37 who, with his sisters, proved a lynch pin of the small pack the College Valley retained in the Second World War: It was a time when 15 couple went out twice a week and, despite the rigors of that period and with little support, they kept the hill farmers happy by killing many a hill fox. A lesson here is surely that, when mated right, a plain out-cross dog of working ability can result in quality hounds just around the corner.

After the tumult of war and the restrictions on fuel were gone, outward investment in hounds was essential, and Ikey Bell, then living in Ireland, noted the performance reputation of the College Valley. He was a weekly letter writer to Goodson and many other innovative masters who pre-war had either taken advantage of the fruits of Ikey's breeding achievements or respected his judgement. It was, therefore, unsurprising that a hard-driving dog, South and West Wilts Lifeguard '44, was the choice since that pack's Godfrey was close up in his tail male background as well as having roots to many lines mentioned in Bell's recently published *Foxhunters Logbook*. Goodson's long-term friendship with the Logans, breeders of the Coniston, and consultation between these two hound men resulted in their choice of Coniston Ringwood '44 to balance the greater orthodoxy of Bell's breeding with Fell hound out-crossing.

However, whether by chance or by pre-meditation, both these dogs had direct tail male linkage to Brecon Paragon

'23, thus implanting close breeding of the most successful bloodline of the 20th century and also linkage to Carmarthen Nimrod '28.

The best products of this strategy were C.V. Legion '49 and C.V. Lawyer '50. Legion '49 was stifled early in his hunting career and was drafted to West Waterford in Eire, where Ikey Bell was lending financial and technical advice to the Morgans, who had boldly assumed mastership of the West Waterford in the immediate post-war years. Legion '49 soon recovered from this injury and proved the schoolmaster of this pack into his 10th season. Then his son West Waterford Guardsman, although a plain but "hunting sound" dog, bred many good hounds. Guardsman was also directly responsible for Ben Hardaway's success with an out-cross for his hard-driving July blood, so well chronicled in his optimistically titled book *Never Out-Foxed*, and thus influential to the modern Crossbred hounds in the USA.

Col. Dick Eames, master of the Cotley, a renowned harrier pack in the West Country, and a keen angler, often on the Tweed, was a friend and admirer of Goodson's post-war hounds and used them frequently to stiffen stamina and drive in his own hounds. This connection was less beneficial in the hills because, although helpful for nose, stamina and drive did not come through in quantity. However Rapid '59, daughter of Cotley Hornet, suffered none of these shortcomings and was lent to the Middleton for accurate hunting ability on the Yorkshire wolds. A gift whelp came back by Middleton Playfair '60, a grandson of Portman Playfair '51, a renowned dog of famous dynasty. Upon maturity, and despite low-country conformation, he showed remarkable nose and accuracy—suitable characteristics for the inexperienced huntsman who had just been appointed to this pack.

C.V. Playfair '63 and his mother, Rapid '59, proved invaluable to the College Valley, and the rising reputation of the West Waterford under Ikey Bell's stewardship produced a gift of Godfrey '61, a grandson of C.V. Legion and of the Pytchley tail female lines respected by Bell. He proved a gift of merit, and mated to Rapid '59 produced a litter of exceptional ability, combining class low country and hill lines. Raglan '66 (see Chapter 16) proved the exceptional working hound of my career, and his brothers and sisters were not far behind. The following season, a gift of United Maple '64, direct tail female to Goodson's foundation bitch Rosebud '21, was put to C.V. Playfair and produced a litter that proved upon maturity to have many of the abilities outlined above.

Thus, throughout the '70s, with our country not yet exposed to shooting pressures, a healthy supply of foxes produced a wealth of sport varied enough to test the hunting ability and further the education of any huntsman, while cementing the evidence of the benefits of out-crossing to lines of established merit. Undue success always stimulates a setback, however, and this came with development of a breeding virus resulting in abortion of whelps and often death of the best potential brood bitches—a disease not unknown today, despite veterinary advances. This resulted in the loss of our original tail female line to Goathland Rosebud, but some good female lines survived with bitches sent away to farms to whelp, and with generous help from the Border Hunt. Development of a new "W" line upon amalgamation with the North Northumberland through Wafer '81 produced a close-scenting family with Old English blood in the background through use of Border Traveller '86 as a sire.

Wager '91 was a late developer, but he led the pack for four seasons with pace and drive, especially during the final stages of a successful hunt. Drafted to Midland USA in his seventh season, he won praise from Ben Hardaway, who wrote in his book that Wager '91 was the only English hound capable of outpacing and out-persevering his July-cross Fell bitches. Wager '91 enjoyed old age with a plethora of willing mistresses. Midland blood was generously returned, particularly so as their donor dispensed the six months of quarantine costs, and those hounds made great contributions in the arid conditions of autumn hunting.

The most successful out-cross with American blood, however, came through a gift from Bill Brainard, MFH of Old Dominion, to Exmoor's MFH Ronnie Wallace. I recall Golden, Old Dominion Gorgeous' daughter, righting the veteran Exmoor hounds on early lambing calls in the late spring with a shrill but melodious cry.

Exmoor Goosestep '83 came to the north as a gift but needed two hill-blood injections to produce sufficient stamina and size to match the benefit of her undoubted nose. Now the great-grand offspring are outstanding for hunting in the modern conditions, where quarry is short and the environment that of heavy stocking and dressed arable land. A Bicester dog, Minstrel '99, with Exmoor Moonstone as grandsire, has produced a large litter mated to this female line that are making an enormous contribution to sport in their eighth season. In the 2003-'04 season, Ian McKie joined the College Valley mastership from the Bicester, which opened doors to Bicester lines that had assisted him as huntsmen of that pack.

My experience over the years encourages me to believe that out-crossing is best applied before shortcomings manifest themselves, not subsequent, so that standards are maintained from a position of strength. Like a well-mixed Live Oak martini cocktail, undue dilution destroys benefit!

I hope this lengthy dissertation in favor of mixing various types of foxhounds is taken as a general tribute to the hound itself, rather than criticism of those following a more conservative approach. This approach has been met with success at the College Valley over a period of 85 years in a testing country, in a pack with long-established female lines—possibly a key ingredient.

I am conscious that there is duplication in this chapter with my epistle on breeding, but repetition also appears in the Bible!

Aboard Misty, one of his favorite hunters, Martin Letts watches hounds draw a covert from a hillside. Rockford is the lone hound.

Crawling among hillside boulders in the mid-'70s, Martin Letts prepares to bolt a fox from a hole, as the College Valley hounds eagerly await their quarry.

Eildon, Martin Letts' wife and joint-master, crossing a College Valley stream on Miss Mustard.

Martin Letts hacking hounds to an early
draw at a 1977 meet.

Ikey Bell (left) and Sir Alfred Goodson were
the two most influential foxhunters of Martin
Letts' life.

Lunchtime while judging a hound show in the
United States.

At the Virginia hound show in the '70s, Martin
Letts (far left) looked eager to get started. Legendary
American masters Ben Hardaway (second left) and
Bill Brainard (far right) were standing by too.

Before a mid-'70s meet, Martin Letts and his
hounds posed in front of the ancient Corbet
Tower, a landmark at the home of Sir Alfred
Goodson, his predecessor as College Valley MFH.

Martin Letts heads his hounds to "a sure find" at
Corbet Tower.

As a young man, Martin Letts (standing, center) often hunted the rivers of Norfolk, Suffolk and Sussex with the Eastern Counties Otterhounds, a pack of mixed varieties of hounds.

C.V. Poacher '72, a strongly built English foxhound, was the most outstanding son of C.V. Raglan '66, Martin Letts' best hound.

Chapter 8

Perseverance

A trait that forms the confidence of the hounds and the reputation of the huntsman.

Many generations of their admirers have debated the various attributes of the foxhound, and arguments over the merits of *pace, drive, nose* and *tongue* have caused many a decanter of port to be emptied around the dinner table. To this may I add *perseverance* and spin an anecdote to justify it?

In the first decade of the 20th century, Alfred Goodson and Nelson Rycroft were commissioned as farm students to a renowned sheep farmer, Mr. Chartres of Akeld farm near Wooler, Northumberland, who was famous for his flock of Cheviot sheep. For payment of £300 they boarded in the farmhouse, received keep for themselves and a hunter, together with stabling. Akeld was a sizeable hill farm of nearly 3,000 acres, employing cattlemen, shepherds, carters for the farm horses, a cobbler and a blacksmith, whose smithy was the reporting place for racing results and foxhunting gossip. Hunting was permissible for the students on a two-day-a-week basis, with an occasional bye. The adjacent North Northumberland Hunt was close, and the Percy and the Duke of Buccleugh were available by railway at £3 for a rail horsebox.

Farmwork was interrupted one day by the cry of hounds, and the Border hounds, hunted by their renowned MFH Jake Robson, appeared over Akeld Hill after a long hunt from Scotland. It was clear a beaten fox had taken refuge in the farm buildings, but search as they may, the hounds, the huntsman and the farm staff could not locate him. So the hounds were called together for the long hack back to the Scottish farm of Attonburn, some 11 miles as the crow flies. Some twenty minutes later, a tremendous squealing rang out from a cottage pigsty, and a search party, with Goodson to the fore, came upon Border Stormer '19 worrying the fox, who had taken refuge behind the sow and her piglets.

When Alfred Goodson started up the College Valley hounds in 1924, with Capt. Claude Lambton, he line-bred his foundation bitches to Stormer's sons Selim '24 and Ringwood and daughters Guilty '22 and Duchess, and he followed this up with Fell out-crosses from Coniston, Blencathra and Eskdale. The perseverance handed down by Stormer manifested itself before the Second World War in the performance of the College Valley hounds, which was recognised by the hunting world pre- and post-war. This persuaded forward-looking masters that these hounds should be eligible for the studbook in the 1950s, so their hunting abilities could be blended with orthodox bloodlines. Prior to that date, Welsh and Fell hounds were excluded and couldn't receive recognition.

Hounds that doggedly refuse to admit defeat, and combine this attribute with drive and fox sense, are particularly valuable to the "let-'em-alone" handlers of hounds. But it can be a drawback once a hound reaches old age, especially in an open riding country, because it cuts the pace as obstinacy overtakes drive. Thus, when talking hounds, over the decanter, perseverance is a quality I search for when looking for an outside dog, for the hound who reinstates the hunt is more invaluable than his brother who runs at head. A dog with such attributes is the one the huntsman looks for at the check. If he is not close up when hounds lose the line, then he will indicate the point of loss more surely than the hard drivers.

I have noticed that upon enquiry of experienced foxhunters as to where hounds checked, at least four different answers are usually forthcoming! It is the point of loss, and the reasons for it, that influence the direction of the cast, and the confidence of the hounds and the reputation of the huntsman each stem upon the success rate of this manoeuvre.

Modern technology—radios, signal collars, mobile phones and such—now have their place in all modern sports and come with advantages, but they do not bring advantage to the practice of woodcraft. In hunting with hounds, early warning of a dangerous situation can speed remedial action, but constant relaying of the whereabouts of the quarry is seriously detrimental to the natural skills of the hounds and the huntsman. It is especially detrimental to the persistence of hounds at the check. If the ringing demand of the telephone too often precedes a regaining of the line, intelligent hounds will cease their own casting ability, and their perseverance wanes.

Chapter 9

Handling Hounds

Stamp your methodology to fulfill your ambitions.

T his is the chapter that has given me the most delay in compiling the anecdotes and reminiscences in this book. Handling hounds in the season is most pertinent to the success of the huntsman and his pack's skills and, thus, reputation. However, it is impertinent to be dogmatic concerning the methodology of handling hounds in the hunting field, as hundreds of men and women work actively to show sport in a varied country, with a variety of quarry, and with the choice of hound they believe is most akin to the district in which they operate. Still, it is always encouraging to the professional to have his own view confirmed, and an increased knowledge about the details of hunting increases everyone's enjoyment of the sport.

The challenge of the regular season is to build upon the education of both the seasoned and the young hounds that you have established during autumn hunting. Also, on the main days, you must satisfy the appetite of the mounted field for forward motion and involve the car contingent so that they feel a positive unit in the process of the day. You can rest assured that some of these priorities do conflict.

The crucial role for a manager in any sport is to develop the players' potential through the best possible practice and to enable them to play as a team, despite the variety of skills they possess. I believe that this precept is not at all wide of the mark for a huntsman. Despite the justifications in my first paragraph, I have been lucky enough to inherit a good pack and to hunt them over quite a period of time. I hope some may find the conclusions of such an experience helpful, but I wish to record than I am not line-bred to Moses and his tabernacles of stone!

There are some days when a good scent causes all the difficulties of our sport to dissipate—usually a combination of a good scent, a degree of luck and sound tactics—but such days are rare. For most days, full concentration, confidence in the hounds and a touch of luck are required to convert a moderate day into a better one, and upon that ability hangs your reputation as a huntsman. A pack where mettle and high fitness are combined does not fully settle the to variables of weather and scent until they become "tuned in" to hunting the quarry, and on an average scenting day this requires twenty minutes or so of continuous hunting.

"Tuned in" is like having a close friend with whom the bumps in friendship are sensibly and easily solved. Many huntsmen will appreciate the advantages of achieving such a start, and they know that when this opportunity is lost through unlucky or ill-managed circumstance, how contagious this becomes as hazards become repetitive and team morale sinks.

In the past, hacking to the meet was a great settling contributor. Lacking that these days, any action that the staff can take to allow hounds to digest the conditions of the day, away from the aroma of excited horses and their riders, is time well spent, especially as modern hunting embraces the meet as an ever-important social occasion. Likewise, a circuitous route to a certain find at the first covert allows a settling period—an opportunity that is often more important for the field than the hounds!

It's tremendously important to remember that horse foil is the worst stain on the land for hounds to hunt through. Field discipline is a factor in controlling that distraction, for confusion seldom achieves success if hounds and horses arrive together.

Always give hounds an ease before venturing in to the first draw. Hounds that arrive at it hot and panting will often miss a fox. If the quarry is soon afoot and circles the extremities of the covert without undue human pressures, hounds are naturally settled, but if he is frustrated or hurried from his chosen direction, the opposite is true. Frank Freeman never touched his horn until his Pytchley fox was away, and no more effective huntsman has existed. Do not compromise a good hunt by noisy encouragement early on.

There is a problem when a good fox goes away from a substantial covert and is holload away by hunt staff or a scout, while the body of the pack is hard at work behind his brother, especially if the direction the fox has taken is an optimum line for a good hunt. Timing is crucial here, for a brief check is the moment to act, especially if you have a helper to hand who has a voice. Intervention, especially early in the day, when experience of the degree of scenting is uncertain, could help hounds. Take a gamble, for, if you fail to act at the proper moment, it could give hounds a signal of uncertainty. And, even if your bold decision meets with failure, another fox may be at home to carry the baton.

Remember, though, that, if hounds naturally fly to your voice after autumn hunting, all options are open—but perseverance suffers if you regularly attempt the impossible.

Any action to assist hounds in sending their quarry away is a combination of timing and instinct, and it will vary with the individual style of the huntsman. When hounds hunt their own fox away on terms, however, they develop a sense of self-achievement and there is a greater chance of dealing successfully with the crucial moments of the day.

The first check in the open is something that can present a problem for the hounds if the scent is at variance between one field and another, especially in intensive farming conditions. It is important not to underestimate the value of a well-placed and sensible scout who lets the fox away from covert at his natural pace, seeing but unseen by the quarry, and then views his route for as long as possible. As a result, the huntsman can choose whether to carry his hounds to the line on clean ground or better still, nudge them forward along the line until a "hit" is achieved. Good recall of the "way" of the fox in past seasons on early mornings is important, as is information especially if accurately and clearly delivered in your preferred methodology. The well-executed nudge without a break in concentration, practiced on early mornings, is of critical assistance toward such handiwork. Such practice will keep your hounds well in touch with your quarry two times out of three, and more often than not it will deliver the conclusive finish so advocated by Ronnie Wallace: "Every hunt should have a beginning, a middle and an ending."

The whipper-in must act in sympathy to the huntsman's style of hunting by combining the cheer with the rate, favoring the former where practical: He must engage tactics to suit the day and its acoustics, judge the severity of the crime before acting, and give the experienced hounds due diligence. A noisy rate to a few upwind of the body of the pack, who are puzzling to hunt on a downwind scent, is a serious distraction, while cheering on the drawing hound from thick covert, when a few hounds have enjoyed a lucky nick in, preserves the valuable attribute of hounds running close as a unit.

Early mornings should develop the teamwork between huntsman and whipper-in, especially how to convey essential and quiet information about hounds and quarry. Tactical hiccups will occur but are best solved at home—an easy maxim to write, but not one I excelled at!

Mr. Jorrocks advocated that the fieldmaster should count to 20 before any action of pursuit, but I would advocate counting to 100, as premature movement of the field all too often stalls the development of a hunt. Premature action results in a muddled start, either through diverting the fox from his chosen route and causing immediate scenting difficulties, by breaking the concentration of the hounds before they are settled to the conditions of the day, or by getting farm stock on the move and adding to the area of foiled ground. The quarry will show his preferred route at a particular point in a covert, but, unless severely balked, will circle and try again. All too often, premature movement by riders discourage this situation and disrupt the quarry's early sortie into open country. If you can achieve a measure of such action on more than a few days, your hounds will be running into "form," an attribute that is self-blossoming and that greatly rewards your pack's reputation.

Casting the hounds when they are substantially at fault is a make-or-break situation, especially if your field is nicely placed at a point of advantage and patiently awaiting fresh action. The huntsman needs to anticipate the causes of a check, and knowing your hounds well will indicate where they lost the line—a vital key in solving the puzzle. Their attention should be gained by voice not horn, and their cast should be achieved voluntarily, without being staff driven. The pace should vary with your summation of the day's conditions, but direction cannot come through the written word. It can only come from our own genius and the confidence between yourself and your hounds!

Close observation assists this skill. Is your quarry a ringer with right-, left- or downwind tendencies? What aspect of foil or farming has halted proceedings, or has sudden shock temporarily halted the scent glands of the pursued? Does wildlife or demeanor of farm stock suggest directional clues, or does a hedgerow conceal some hidden hindrance? If forward is your best option, consider an insurance cast back and assess which direction hounds covered inadequately in their initial self-casting. Indecision in such matters must not be signalled to the pack, and the pace of remedial action should be conducted while keeping the scenting conditions of the hour in mind. Send on a scout to fish out likely information, and have your field stationary just short of where hounds checked, until you signal—the most sure way to lose the quarry is to permit the field to accompany the huntsman in his cast.

Fieldmastering is a skill beyond my remit, but it should combine the skill of horsemanship and houndsmanship. An intelligent go-between acting between huntsman and fieldmaster is a vital role, especially when information about the quarry disintegrates the carefully planned draw, or the huntsman adapts a silent mode, as we all do! If farming or shooting relations require a halt to a fine hunt, make sure it is achieved sympathetically and take time to "fuss" the hounds.

Sooner or later, your luck will run out, and the pack will lose form. Do not stick rigidly to traditions—of dogs or bitches, Wednesday or Saturday location—but apply innovation. Vary the players, and reduce the pack size in favor of experience. There will be days when "over-viewing," riot or blank draws unsettle the hounds. Arrange a bye day and take them to a well-foxed woodland, curtail help to the late afternoon, and the hunt of a lifetime may develop! During such a spell of ill luck or bad handling with the College Valley, I telephoned Johnnie Richardson of the Blencathra. "Grin and bear it, Martin," was his succinct solution, but I replied that I had never excelled at either! I have noticed that the professionals surpass the amateurs in this respect. We all have a purple patch in the season, but must never take success for granted. Instead, we must apply the same principles of observation, concentration and methodology as vigorously as we do on opening day.

Perhaps these notes overemphasize the handling of the independent hound, but this is the direction where my experience lies, and this direction has led to the development of an intellectual hound that has assisted a range of packs across the world.

Those who have had the lucky experience of working with a true woodsman, whose tracking and stalking skills are exceptional, will appreciate that his skills come from an uncluttered mind and a lifetime of working in a wild and unspoilt environment, one that requires him to apply his attributes on very frequent occasion. But you will be a very lucky client indeed if he can repair your vehicle or mend your camping utensils! Such people have a very high respect for the quarry, and those who pursue dangerous animals never take their reactions for granted. In fact, they usually bear the scars of some misread exploit. If you possess such a man in your neighborhood, give him full attention.

Chapter 10

Get Off To A Good Start

It will certainly boost the pack's morale.

High-class teams of sportsmen know the value of a good start—seventy-five runs on the board before the first wicket falls, or two goals in the first twenty minutes, raises morale to a level from which the opposition seldom recovers. This applies to a team, a pack or a horse.

In order to get off to a good start during autumn hunting, give considerable thought to picking a good location for the first few mornings, one where a litter of foxes is in residence and located in a sizeable wood where thick trees are balanced with glades. This allows the tail of the pack to naturally get up to the head when the quarry turns short, and infrequent viewing of their quarry keeps the pack on their noses. Quiet hunting information is vital for the huntsman to make these first few mornings invaluable. Such information extends the option of a nudge so that hounds either sense self-achievement and are stimulated into repeat performance, or, alternatively, advances the option of stronger direction, which gains their confidence in their huntsman's abilities to help them.

Four or five mornings of success in such locations will do wonders for the young hounds and also the first-season hounds who, through injury, are short of experience. But do not squander such a start by going too often to small coverts, where viewing and holding up stimulate over-excitement. It is only common sense to vary location to ensure a mix of assistance or non-assistance, thus ensuring concentration of the whole pack. A good-scenting morning can encourage a long day of sport, but the interests of the young hounds and their enthusiasm should be a higher priority than testing the stamina of the experienced hounds and extending the tally. It is never a mistake to go home early on a good note.

If a difficult spell develops, reduce the number of hounds in the field, alter the ratio of the experienced to the young, and leave the possible troublemakers at home—they have the season before them. Every entry has its late starters, but it is my experience that the stars develop from that section of the pack, rather than from the precocious.

Whenever appropriate, never turn down the opportunity to hunt out a stale line, particularly in the open. It is an invaluable opportunity to evaluate your pack's perseverance, and should it develop into a fresh find and a successful finish, it is more valuable than several good-scenting mornings in succession.

Autumn hunting and its methodology are as vital to hounds as schooling is to the child. The skills of perseverance and venery learned in youth are almost more important to the fashionable pack, where the desire for galloping runs has to impinge on the need for the advantage of a long but slow hound hunt. If shooting pressures necessitate a visit to an estate where the quarry is in short supply, leave the young entry at home. Into October give the pack experience of hunting at a later hour, for the opening meet is not the best date to present hounds with the difficulties of a hot and scentless midday, along with greatly increased horse foil, unless they already have the experience to deal with it.

Chapter 11

Breeding Reminiscences

The men and hounds who've taught me the most.

Luck, undoubtedly, plays a tremendously important, but under-appreciated, role in hound breeding, so what a wonderful measure of chance it was that Ikey Bell's education at Cambridge exposed a weakness in a particular subject. His tutors strongly recommended a "crammer" (extra tuition) to remedy it, and Walter Rawnsley, in the Southwold country, was the choice. He provided a sporting household where experimental practice on the hunting horn was tolerated. But it was especially lucky that Walter's cousin was Preston Rawnsley, master of the Southwold and an experienced breeder of hounds.

Under Preston's tutelage, Bell's education in foxhunting was greatly advanced—in extension of pedigrees, in kennel management through visits to the home pack and to the adjacent Brocklesby, and in hound management courtesy of Charlie Gilson, kennel huntsman to the Southwold hounds at that time. So much time was devoted to these studies that the gap in education remained unclosed and Bell was sent down from Cambridge the following term. But he then persuaded his mother to take a hunting box in Melton and hunted six days a week in The Shires with all the famous packs—a form of education from which the foxhunting world has greatly benefited throughout his lifetime and beyond, despite this lack of scholarship.

The advantage of youth is that learning ability is at its height, and I was extremely lucky to join Sir Alfred Goodson in the mastership of the College Valley in my thirtieth year. I was already aware of the hunting skills of his unique pack, but, alas, I was too green to fully appreciate the opportunities afforded by this event. In my first year in the North, I followed hounds on my feet, but in the '64-65 season I hunted hounds mainly on (but often off) a horse: Although I was piloted by Eildon, my wife, my mount Jess, a Thoroughbred mare, was often forced to navigate the bogs wherever, in ignorance, I took her.

Sir Alfred was convinced that all that was required for a good day's hunting was to take his hounds to the meet and let them do the rest. Nevertheless, at the end of my first season we agreed that more accuracy and nose should be a concentration for future breeding, as there was drive-a-plenty. Sir Alfred was a skilled breeder of cattle, sheep, game fowl, pigeons, bantams and hounds, but part of that skill was consulting with the stockmen and drawing out their knowledge of all the species he worked with, including his inexperienced huntsman. He possessed one prejudice against the modern English foxhound, which he described as "Wallyitis"—waiting, head in the air, at the check for help from the huntsman, a trait he imagined displayed by the orthodox hounds, especially those handled by Capt. Ronnie Wallace.

Lord Halifax, master of the Middleton, had borrowed a bitch, College Valley Rapid '59, with an exceptional nose and a Harrier background, and a gift whelp came back, a hound whose grandsire was the famous Portman Playfair '51. This dog, Playfair '63, played a noticeable part at the check during his first season, particularly on a moderate scent. Having a star like this among the pack influences the body to hunt more in his style, a trait that is particularly noticeable at marking. Playfair threw plain dogs but quality bitches and, mated to Blencathra Ruby '65, he bred an influential dog, Ringwood '69. A mark of an outstanding hound is how widespread he can transmit his influence.

Pedigree research also revealed that we were running low on Sir Alfred's original foundation bitch tail line, from Goathland Rosebud '21. So Sir Alfred called upon his great friend John Yeoward, who had been successful at upgrading the United hounds in hill country on the Welsh borders. John had proved a very useful mole in Wales, digging up good Welsh lines and crossing these with College Valley-bred gifts, which on request for merit then came back to home base. United Maple '64 was an outstanding example, and she proved an accurate hunter. Maple '64 was a granddaughter of C.V. Magic '51 whose name was appropriate for her abilities and who possessed the female line to Rosebud '21. Mated to Playfair '63 she brought up an outstanding litter of eight hounds.

In Ireland Ikey Bell was helping Tom and Elsie Morgan, the masters of the West Waterford. The Morgans were brilliant at crossing a hairy country in sporting style, and Elsie had acquired hunting skills in early life through whipping in to Pat Thatcher at the Llangibby during the Second World War. Ikey was determined to breed a pack worthy of the Morgans' keenness and hunting skills. C.V. Legion '49 crossed the channel and mated to West Cumberland Guilty '54. Ikey had purchased this bitch in the Fells, because her reputation was high for sagacity, and she proved that his eye for a good cross was undiminished. West Waterford Godfrey '61, a grandson of Legion, came back to us as a return gift, and although not a striking dog to look at, he proved his worth in the field. The litter, including four tough dogs, one of whom, Raglan '66, was the outstanding dog of my career as a huntsman (see

Chapter 16). Thus, two substantial litters, entered in the mid '60s, had great influence on the performance of the College Valley throughout the '70s and beyond.

How are these examples of breeding in the late '60s relevant today? Firstly, perhaps the element of luck was present, because I could not at all claim experience in such matters. Secondly, the value of friendship and generosity in the hunting world is as relevant today as in the past, where loan of hounds from countries of similar terrain and hunting style can fulfill your ambitions. Thirdly, if you spot a weakness in your own hounds, take concentrated action to close it by seeking help from a pack with a strong reputation in the attributes you seek. Either dogs or bitches are beneficial vehicles for use, but a good bitch is often more readily available.

If their pedigree background co-opts similar blood to your favorite home lines and combines the best blood of established premier packs, then there are extra advantages. If you can use bitches of proven mothering ability, you are more likely to achieve a healthy litter, and this comes down the line in succeeding generations. A caveat in this is not to unduly test a bitch capable of raising a very large litter—it narrows the gene pool and may affect her ability to run up later in life.

When selecting an outside dog or bitch, always inquire about the merits of the family, for if you tap in to one where general merit and longevity are well spread, you are better rewarded than going for a one-off genius. Don't be too disappointed if a visiting dog does not fulfil his reputation at home in the field. A move from home base is a traumatic experience for an intelligent hound. I was given a dog of high reputation who didn't perform until the following season, although some of my friends label me as unfriendly in the hunting field! A dog who proves successful across a variety of packs of hounds is also a signal of a great sire, and a recovered attribute that has worked for others is surely more likely to work for you.

If you achieve early success, do not lay claim to green-fingered ability. Instead, keep working away at your home blood, bringing in outside refreshers, and remember to breed—first, second and third—for work. Quality is a bonus that will inevitably appear, but be prepared to wait a generation or three for its arrival. If a pack of 35 couple suits your length of pocket, maintain the balance of your pack to accommodate the various ages up to the sixth or seventh seasons. Do not flood the kennel with a particular entry, no matter how good-looking they are. Lines that run up late in life are very precious indeed, as they solve many problems for the huntsman, should he be man (or woman) enough to admit it!

An added challenge arrived in the early '80s, when the College Valley Hunt amalgamated with the North Northumberland. This union greatly increased the need for versatility in the pack, as most of the acquired country was arable, with the odd large wood. Sheep farming in the hills required hounds to cull the foxes to secure a successful lambing, while the arable country required greater accuracy and perseverance without loss of pace. Specialized hounds will excel in their accustomed territory, but surely a signal of high merit is when they do well on unaccustomed terrain.

The solution, I determined, should come through the original College Valley lines, with the introduction of the best North Northumberland female line. This proved, after a season, to be the "W" line, with a Cotswold and Old English base. In addition, I used a gift from the Exmoor, bringing the wonderful American line, Old Dominion Gorgeous, which Ronnie Wallace had developed from an initial gift from its renowned master, Bill Brainard.

An amalgamation is a difficult move for traditional packs to accept—particularly in Northumberland, perhaps the most non-change county in England. However, lady luck played her part, and two outstanding hunts happened in early

November—a five mile point on the arable country with a spectacular finish in the River Tweed and, on the following Saturday, a six-mile point into the hills with a successful finish. This confounded the pessimists and enthused the optimists, further evidence that success in sports always cements changes.

Blencathra Glider '76, perhaps the best Fell hound bred by Johnnie Richardson at Blencathra, was used by Tim Unwin successfully at the Cotswold and bore out the maxim that a great hound's progeny will perform in any country. This hound, because of his College Valley tail male background, seemed an obvious option to upgrade my North Northumberland "W" female line, and that union produced Sailor '83, a very able stallion hound, and some very hard-working sisters.

Like the aforementioned refresher dogs of the late '60s, Glider's progeny proved outstanding, and fresh finance from a combined source allowed more generous entries. Success came again from the United hunt with the importation of two outstanding bitches, Rollo and Ladybird, when Rodney Ellis retired as master, and they enabled a fresh injection of nose and drawing ability.

With the approach of the 21st century, I was rising three score years and ten and my abilities to ride up with my hounds was on the wane, despite Eildon's ability to find an able hill horse at a moderate price. However, an independent pack and knowledge of the country enabled many hunts to be successfully concluded at the trot, as my hounds showed every sign of sympathy for my old age!

My last throw of luck was that Ian McKie, master of the Bicester and Whaddon Chase, had expressed an interest in taking a pack in the North. He and his wife, Tocky, subsequently purchased a sporting estate at Lanton, and Ian became a joint master and huntsman. This happy arrangement produced all the out-crossing possibilities of the Bicester, carefully nurtured for the last 35 years by the two Ians—Farquhar and McKie—as an added bonus.

I am flattered that many packs, both in England and in America, find that the College Valley blood assists their hunting abilities, despite their specializing in a wild country. Experience has taught me that, as in many sports, maintaining high standards over the years requires much more research and work than winning a short-term reputation, however successful.

Chapter 12

Heaven Is Close

Especially on Holy Island.

On the northeast coast of Northumberland lies a sand bar, and at its end exists a small island, consisting of sand dunes and pasture, known as Holy Island. In the 7th century St. Cuthbert selected this location as a haven of peace and comparative safety from which to extend Christianity among the lawless Northumbrian society of rogues and ruffians who frequented that wild moorland along the sea coast. It was here that the famous Gospels were inscribed in copperplate writing and beautifully illustrated, setting out the conditions of Christianity in order to qualify for a long existence and a happy afterlife in heaven.

In subsequent times, the monastery became a source of pilgrimage, and eventually a village grew around the monastery, complete with two inns licensed to cater to the welfare of a few hundred population and the visiting pilgrims. In the 1980s drinking and driving became a frowned-on practice, and whenever the tides made the causeway on the connecting sand bar impassable, the inn was chosen as a popular venue for late-night parties or after-hours drinking, because police attention was impracticable. Holy Island was also the first landfall for birds migrating to these shores for a milder winter than their birthplace in Scandinavia. Foxes crossed the causeway to thrive upon these migrant birds, weary after a hazardous sea trip of many hundreds of miles.

The warden of this bird sanctuary grasped the nettle of his conflicting convictions, and eventually he reconsidered his love of nature and his hunting prejudices. He agreed to a degree of culling of the fox population in the interest of birdlife, provided hunting was pursued in a low-key style. Thus, on a very frosty morning, eight riders, dressed in ratcatcher, assembled at mid-tide with 12 ½ couple of foxhounds and waited for the tide to close over the causeway. Foxes were mostly an un-enterprising lot on the island, since their quarry was readily to hand, but after a number of local scurries, a good fox set off in determined manner to circle the sand bar on the fringe of the island. On most days the sand carried little scent, but today hounds drove on with good cry, a cry re-echoed when a flock of Brent geese were flushed by the fox and then by the foxhounds. A holloa raised the pack's heads for a moment, and, after spotting the splashes made by the fox along the sea's edge, they quickly overhauled a tired fox.

Returning to Wooler, the huntsman, with face flushed by an icy wind and a successful bye day snatched from the weather, met a disgruntled subscriber who growled, "And where the hell have you been hunting today, Martin?"

"Holy Island," was the response.

"Well, that's the nearest you'll ever get to heaven!" he said, with a half-smile. He may have had a point!

An after-thought to this hunt occurred later to me: How did hounds recognize the significance of splashes in the sea, when their experience of such happenings was limited to once in a lifetime?

Chapter 13

Turn Of The Tide

A tale of misadventure at the heavenly host.

I f you wish to frequently entertain visitors, it is very helpful to have good livery stables within the borders of your country, establishments that can provide suitable hunters acclimatized to the terrain within it. We have a shining example of this particular luxury in our country, run by a couple who are each knowledgeable on hunting and wise about horses. But, like most stockmen, they are no mechanics. Their horsebox, with brand name proudly emblazoned on its tailgate, was a difficult vehicle to overtake, as the black smoke it invariably exuded from its exhaust pipe destroyed the vision of oncoming vehicles!

Dickie was a member of a large family, and nearly all were keen hunters, as their father was a well-known master and huntsman and a friend and admirer of Sir Alfred Goodson. They achieved summer income through riding lessons and summer rides—the most popular feature being rides on the shores of Holy Island, with the sands providing fine natural gallops and affording swimming in the sea. On these occasions white shirts raised the libido of the proprietor to dangerous levels when moist, feeding his interest in human as well as equine make and shape.

His elder sister, well known for creating order out of chaos in the classroom but chaos out of order in the hunting field, trained an eventer with an unreasonable dislike for the water feature. On the eve of an event with this type of obstacle in the early stages of the course, Dickie, with his sister's agreement, selected her horse to lead a beach ride. They had made the not unreasonable assumption that the sea, with no obstacles, might preclude problems on course the next day. All started well, as the visitors swam their hirelings, but then the ladies' clothes became more transparent, and Dickie rode to the rescue, with appropriate applause for his chivalry, of a blonde who had ventured into the deep.

All too quickly, though, it was time to return to the horsebox, suitably parked on the causeway at low-tide level. A canter to it seemed appropriate but led by the eventer, highly fed for his next expedition and eager to put distance from his water phobia, the pace improved to a rapid gallop. Most of the horses slowed appropriately at the horsebox, but the blonde recipient of Dickie's best hireling galloped on with a main road and railway line as close hazards. Dickie, of course, set off in pursuit, and if it wasn't for a boggy field with a pond, farce might have descended to fatality.

The lady's hysterics took some time to subside, despite close encouragement, and the pair returned to find all the horses loaded in the horsebox, with the rising tide lapping round the wheels. Dickie's application of the key to unlock the cab was so urgent that it broke in the car door handle, so, an urgent unloading was followed by retreat to dry land across the flooding causeway, before the spare horsebox was summoned from base. Salt water was no catalyst to the temperamental engine, and an already rusted chassis suffered permanent decline, along with the engine. Luckily the father of the blonde was a garage proprietor, and a deal for an alternative was struck after much lengthy, and intimate, negotiation.

Alas, the eventer was not freshened by the traumas of the day, and he collapsed in the coffin jump just prior to the water the next day. He took some time to extract—enough time, in fact, for the local press to film the occurrence. Unfortunately for Josephine, the owner, who had claimed sickness to miss school and attend the event, her headmaster spotted the footage and firmly told her the following day that if she was going to skip school, she should not be filmed doing it!

Dickie didn't feel the need to fully brief his sister on the reasons behind the eventer's sudden loss of form, but, unfortunately for him, the loss of any vehicle on the tidal causeway has always excited the local press. The prominent tailboard was clearly visible in the press photo, easily exposing his indiscretion. Family relations were only restored on the condition of the departure of one good and handsome customer, along with discounted livery costs for the eventer!

There was, however, no need to bother the local scrap merchant about the horsebox. When the generous tide flooded in, it lifted the chassis gently off the ground, and, aided by a strong current, it floated on off to oblivion.

Chapter 14

Robert's Fox

A hard frost revealed a memorable hunt,
until darkness fell.

At times of snow and frost, many of our neighboring packs stay in their kennels, but the College Valley hounds are used to such conditions, and we've had some of our best days during hard weather. That was the case in 1967-'68, when hunting was closed from November to February, but our hounds hunted successfully immediately, despite the snow and frost that set in shortly after hunting had resumed. And such a day was a Saturday in February 1988 when, after a hard frost, the snowdrifts lay in hard white streaks about the hill faces and the tracks and river bottoms were iron-hard. Fortunately there was much forestry and rough ground in Bowmont Water, where the frost could not penetrate, so the meet was on.

On moving off, there was more than one fox afoot, which necessitated stopping one section of the pack to pursue the main body, which was taking a more likely route. Just as this was achieved, it became clear that my hunt secretary, leading an offshoot group of riders, had substantially headed the fox, just as a hunt appeared to be developing. His excuses fell on more stony ground than the conditions underfoot, and this was reinforced when it was apparent the fox had turned back into a covert, which was the site I'd planned for my afternoon draw. Once again, fresh foxes split the pack, thus adding to my instincts of lost opportunity. Hounds struggled for some time in a forestry block—usually the graveyard to many a good hunt—until eventually a good holloa signalled a fox away in the right direction. The weight of cry drew all the pack behind the right fox.

After crossing Bowmont Water, the fox turned short about the edge of the Duke of Roxburgh's trees, an indication that he was out of his accustomed territory and that we were in for a long hunt. When hit by hard weather, the shepherd brings his sheep off the hill ground onto turnips or feed pasture, and our fox's next move was to turn through a flock of ewes held up in this way, so the pack had to hunt through the heavily foiled ground, with the sheep moving back to the hill before them. Their perseverance was eventually rewarded when they reached clean ground and drove on to Craikmoor. Into the next valley they ran, with the cream of the Border country before them, but with increasing hill fog hanging on the high ground.

"Go on, go on," was my instruction to our small team of motor-bikers—Robert, James and Robby—as only they could keep up with the racing pack in this steep and frozen country. At last hounds checked on the scree of the Callowhope in descending gloom. Returning frost and many miles from home seemed to make closure a sensible option, but seven couple were on with the fox, and their increasing cry made me again question caution. As the horses were done after a hunt of 15 miles, we turned for home as I instructed Robert to keep with the hounds and stop them when opportunity presented itself. As we regained our hunt boundary, more hounds rejoined us showing signs of success, and Robert soon confirmed that hounds had overhauled a barren vixen in a rush-bed at Peelienic, just below the English border, 8

½ miles as the crow flies from the find. Thus a hazardous ride home down a frosted track became a pleasure, despite the Galloway cattle blowing at us with frosted breath and horses slipping and sliding in pitch darkness to our vehicles, parked at Belford.

Never was a dram of whisky and a fire at the Border Hotel more welcome and more able to stimulate individual stories of a memorable day. Alas, the secretary and his chastened group went home early and missed the hunt. Was it rubbing salt into verbal wounds to give him the details of memorable hunt and our adventures? After consideration, I thought so.

Chapter 15

Baking Day

"Dispatch that fox, or you'll not eat!"

Cocklawfoot was a hill farm in Bowmont Valley owned by the Duke of Roxburgh and managed by John Elliot. For many years it was herded by three members of the Little family, all keen foxhunters, and two of them possessors of Highland-cross ponies that were ideal dual-purpose mounts—to herd the sheep and to follow hounds. They were fair-minded about the fox, which was encouraged in winter but a staunch foe at lambing time, when a rogue could cause an inordinate amount of extra work at a very busy time.

The Littles always kept a pig, which was slaughtered in November to restock the larder when blizzards might curtail the flow of essential foods. A successful meet in their locality at that time always elicited an invitation from Mary Little, their widowed mother, to a delicious hunting tea, one which included excellent broth, many types of scone, and perhaps a dram. An autumn meet, timed to coincide with slaughter of the pig and homemade sausage production, was therefore not to be missed.

In the '70s such a day was arranged, and a good hunt developed in the afternoon, as a stout hill fox took us over the main Cheviot ridge and finished in the late afternoon at an earth deep in the Border hunt country, having achieved a seven-mile point. A long dig was scorned, and with thoughts of sausages gently browning in a pan, the long hack to Cocklawfoot proceeded at a pace.

On reaching Cocklawfoot, we were surprised to see Mary Little, girded in a large apron with lower arms whitened by flour, looking hot and bothered. It transpired that a fox hunted by one hound had taken refuge in the hay barn, and its future welfare was not high in Mrs. Little's order of priorities. So baking was suspended and the exit blocked by her formidable figure waving an apron. Feeble excuses from myself on our return after a long hack home—such as a hard day for hounds and for horses—were not acceptable, and her condition for future hospitality ever again was action from a terrier and the assembled pack. The fox soon bolted and eventually succumbed after a local scurry about the farm and nearby wood, despite many twists and turns about the wall tops and buildings. And the hunt finished appropriately at Mary's feet. She pronounced this was the best hunt of her lifetime, and sausages were duly served for tea, as well as two drams.

It was well dark when we drove back to Wooler and our house beyond, and we came upon two dinner guests inquiring the way to our house from a bystander. "Follow the horn," was my instruction, "but dinner will be late."

Chapter 16

Raglan '66

My most brilliant hound.

Raglan '66 was the best dog of the best litter I had the good fortune to hunt in my early years as a huntsman. He was the best of an outstanding litter by Playfair '63 and out of Maple '64, a litter that I have previously mentioned.

Raglan was the last hound to be walked at a very hospitable farm called Attonburn, in Bowmont Water. Two pots of soup simmered continually on the Aga—one for the family and guests and the other for the innumerable Collies and hound pups. When offered some soup in the kitchen, it was advisable to test its aroma to ensure it came from the right pot! Perhaps Raglan's supremacy at walk was that he had occasionally benefited from the contents of the human pot! He came from a litter of seven: four dogs and three bitches. Two succumbed quickly (one to a dislodged boulder on a scree face), and we sent Ransome to the USA, as a present to Bill Brainard, the master of the Old Dominion in Virginia.

In those days I kept a spare page in my pedigree book to write a working report on each hound's season, a good practice for reference that only lapsed when pressures of organization prevented me from updating it. Recent historical revision revealed that Raglan was noted as an outstanding fox catcher. In the 1967-'68 season, hounds were confined to kennel from mid-November to February 1 due to a foot-and-mouth epidemic. Foxes, therefore, were unusually plentiful in the winter, despite the weather, so hounds quickly hit form and caught 20 brace between that date and mid-April. Raglan was so often close up at the finish that his muzzle resembled that of a hard-bitten terrier, but with greater experience he developed a better grip!

Ranter, his brother, also had a keen nose, but since he had a straighter shoulder, he possessed less pace. In his fourth season, Ranter was drafted to the Cotley and displayed sufficient prowess to catch the attention of Martin Scott at Tiverton, so he sired some very good hounds. Raglan's two sisters were also stars: One was hard-driving and the other low-scenting, a useful combination.

Raglan continued to excel until the end of his fourth season and was noted for his ferocity at the kill or mark. His last day was in Langleeford, a valley owned by Lord Astor and farmed by the Brown family, all keen hunters. Foxes were often driven downwind out of College Valley into this location, and Matty Little and Jim Matheson, or the Brown family, often shepherded hounds over the main road between Wooler and Powburn when rough terrain delayed the huntsman.

At the end of March, we met at Langleeford and later on found a stout fox. The fox circled the high ground, and by the cry I judged that the hounds were close up when the fox ran past the meet to climb the 1,500 feet to Cheviot by the Scald Hill and Hooley Crag, so named to describe the northwestern wind whistling through this rock outcrop. Cheviot is too steep and boggy to ride, so the tactic is to skirt its flank, and nine times out of ten a nick in can be achieved when a tired fox descends down the gullies of the Bizzle or Hen Hole. Halfway down to the former, I heard my wife's "who-oop" re-echoed by the Coldburn scree. As I passed Raglan, stretched out near a burn, I received two waves of his stern in recognition, but, having broken up the fox, I went back to find him dead. His loss was a hard blow, but no more fitting an end could come for an exceptional hound who had been close up at the finish of many a hunt.

Fortunately, Raglan had been mated to a bitch, a gift from the Duke of Beaufort, by Heythrop Cockspur out of Posy '63, a Peterborough champion by their famous Palmer '59. This venture into distinguished blood produced improved quality and accurate hunting, especially in the only dog, Poacher '72, who was as rich also in intellect but without Raglan's fire and brilliance. However, he passed his attributes to the many local packs who used him, and his sisters were each good enough to use. The best, Posy, was brilliant at re-finding the fox whenever he adopted an unusual refuge, and she achieved this when on loan to the Blencathra. Johnnie Richardson admired this talent, and her line is respected there to this day.

It is seldom easy, in my experience, to reproduce extreme brilliance in hounds, but to stimulate general performance, it must be a route to follow.

Raglan's photo had pride of place in a pocket of my wallet for many years, but after extreme wear my wife substituted it for a picture of herself. I thought it diplomatic not to re-arrange her gift.

ABOUT THE AUTHOR

The legendary Martin Letts was the MFH and huntsman of England's College Valley Hunt for almost fifty years, developing a revered pack of foxhounds that have been influential in packs throughout England and the USA. Few people alive today know more about hounds or hunting than he does.